STARTING A RESURGENT AMERICA: SOLUTIONS

DESTABILIZED AMERICA, ECONOMY, TRADE POLICY, SOCIAL SECURITY, MEDICARE, OBAMACARE, EDUCATION, CHILD CARE, IMMIGRATION, REVIVING INDUSTRY, CRIME, SECURITY, TERRORISM, PRISONS, POVERTY, UNEMPLOYMENT, MEDIA EXCESSES, EXPORTING TECHNOLOGY, POLLUTION, WASTE DISPOSAL, SPACE, RESEARCH, AND DEFENSE

STEPHEN BLAHA, PH. D.

JANUS ASSOCIATES INC. (NH)

ISBN: 978-0-9845530-8-2

Federal and state legislators, and government officials, are given permission to make paper copies of any, or all, parts of this book for the use of their staffs and colleagues.

Cover Credits
Cover by Stephen Blaha © 2013.

Rev. 00/00/01   March 31, 2013

To My Wife Margaret

Some Other Books by Stephen Blaha

SuperCivilizations: Civilizations as Superorganisms (McMann-Fisher Publishing, Auburn, NH, 2010)

The Rhythms of History: A Universal Theory of Civilizations. Pingree-Hill Publishing. Auburn, NH, 2002).

The Life Cycle of Civilizations. (Pingree-Hill Publishing. Auburn, NH, 2002).

A Unified Quantitative Theory of Civilizations and Societies: 9600 BC - 2100 AD (Pingree-Hill Publishing, Auburn, NH, 2004).

Bright Stars, Bright Universe (Pingree-Hill Publishing, Auburn, NH, 2009).

To Far Stars and Galaxies: Second Edition of Bright Stars, Bright Universe (Pingree-Hill Publishing, Auburn, NH, 2009).

All the Universe! Faster Than Light Tachyon Quark Starships & Particle Accelerators with the LHC as a Prototype Starship Drive Scientific Edition (Pingree-Hill Publishing, Auburn, NH, 2011).

Multi-Stage Space Guns, Micro-Pulse Nuclear Rockets, and Faster-Than-Light Quark-Gluon Ion Drive Starships (Blaha Research, Auburn, NH, 2013).

Available on Amazon.com, Amazon.co.uk, bn.com and other web sites as well as at better bookstores (through Ingram Distributors).

Preface

The recent elections have focused on negatives: how to cut programs and how to raise taxes. The discussions in the Presidential debates and in Congressional contests were oriented to the issues of what programs to cut, what programs not to cut, who should get tax increases and who should get tax relief.

The debates did not focus on the root causes behind the need for cutbacks and increased taxes: the decline in the American economy – a decline largely caused by a multi-decade trade imbalance fed by an unfair trade policy of low import duties, and the relatively high level of American workers' wages compared to foreign wages. The granting of "Most Favored Nation" status to China in the early 1990's, together with China's extraordinary low average wages and China's robber baron attempts to capture major industries such as pharmaceuticals, have led to a massive trade imbalance with China that has enabled it to increase its defense expenditures and economy to a level near that of the United States. This development mirrors the economic tragedy of Rome where Chinese silk was bought in large quantity with Roman gold leading to the debasement of Roman currency, and the Roman Empire's economy, (sound familiar?) just as the currency of the United States is being debased – inflation, the elimination of silver coinage, and the change of the copper content of nickels. (A nickel – five cents – now costs the US Treasury eleven cents to manufacture.)

Perhaps this situation, unmentioned in the Presidential debates, represents a desire of both political parties to exchange American dollars for Chinese cooperation in world affairs – a form of bribery that our forefathers rejected in the war with the Mediterranean Barbary pirates, "Millions for defense. Not one cent for Tribute." Perhaps there is a fear of the Chinese sale of a trillion dollars of Treasury bonds.

In any case the core problem of the American economy was not addressed – only its symptoms such as the US budget deficit.

In this book we will address the issues mentioned in the book's title and make specific proposals for their solution. The American economy and government is declining with foreign trade the core problem. We will not suggest Protectionism. Protectionism was tried before the Great Depression and found to worsen the world's economy. We will suggest a gradual program to dampen foreign opportunism and restore the American economy with low unemployment, a revived industrial base, and a strong program to help Americans in need.

One might ask how this author can engage in the consideration of the issues presented in this book. The author has been a student of world history for over fifty years and in recent years has developed the most detailed study of world civilizations since Toynbee. A study of over fifty civilizations is described in books from *The Rhythms of History* (2002) to Supercivilizations: Civilizations as Superorganisms (2010). His theory successfully accounts for the rise and fall of civilizations. In particular, his theory of Classic Mayan civilization closely matches its rises and falls and is very consistent with the latest studies of Central American rainfall patterns. America, together with the rest of Western civilization, is undergoing a decline according to this theory that will reach bottom in 2048.

A major initiative by the American people can stem or mitigate this decline. With that hope we proceed to consider its problems and propose concrete solutions to end the decline.

CONTENTS

1. THE FUNDAMENTAL PROBLEM: THE DECLINE OF AMERICAN INDUSTRY DUE TO A RUINOUS TRADE POLICY 1

The Problems Created by a Seriously Adverse Trade Imbalance 2
A possible Solution Based on Creating a Tariff Structure Based on Wage Differentials between Countries 4
Outsourcing Work to Foreign Countries 7
Additional Cutbacks in the Outflow of US Dollars...........................8
Benefits for America and Its Trading Partners 10
Possible Problems Resulting from the Proposed Tariff Structure....12
Chinese and Indian Resistance? 14
    China.. 14
    India... 17
How long can China Play its North Korean Card?..........................17

2. A DESTABILIZED AMERICA...19

Instability in the Lives of the People 20
Instability in Government 22
Instability of the Future America...24
    Increasing Demands for Support from the People................................... 24
    Higher Small Business Barriers 25
    "Bread and Circuses" America?.. 25
    Growth of Corruption.. 26
    US Trend to a Third World Raw Materials Economy............................... 26
    Population Trends 27
    Hope for America! 27

3. SOCIAL SECURITY, MEDICARE, AND OBAMACARE 28

Social Security 28

Medicare 29

Ways of Reducing Medicare Outlays Gracefully 30

Obamacare 32

Economic Benefit of Medicare, Social Security, and Federal
Employment 35

4. EDUCATION..36

How can We Improve Education? 38

At The School Level 38

At the National Level 39

5. IMMIGRATION 42

The Question of Illegal Immigrants 44

Preventing New Illegal Immigration............................45

6. MEDIA EXCESSES 48

Television 49

Movies 51

Other Media 51

The Blurred Line between Reality and the Media.........51

Eighty Years of Brain Washing 52

7. CRIME, SECURITY, TERRORISM, AND PRISONS 54

Criminal Activity 54

Drugs and Crime - Legalization...................................55

Freeing the Drug Addicts in Prison 57

The Cost of Prisons 57

Terrorists...60

Prison Abuses 61

A Major Misconception about Prisons 61

Excess Federal Appeals by Criminals 62

8. POVERTY AND UNEMPLOYMENT 63

Poverty in America 63

Can we Remedy Poverty?...64

The Rumford Solution for the Poor 65

Help the Children 66

Help Families 67

Unemployment in America 67

Who Pays for these Programs 68

9. POLLUTION AND WASTE DISPOSAL 69

Is there a Solution? 70

The Price 71

The Benefits 71

10. EXPORTING TECHNOLOGY 73

11. SPACE, RESEARCH, AND DEFENSE 76

Space 76

Research 78

Defense 78

POSTSCRIPT 80

REFERENCES 81

INDEX 83

ABOUT THE AUTHOR 85

1. The Fundamental Problem: The Decline of American Industry Due to a Ruinous Trade Policy

Most times, in the history of nations, great nations have declined for great reason. However, in some cases the fall of great nations has been precipitated by seemingly minor events that grow to engulf the prosperity and strength of the nation.

In the 1980's trade with China, and underdeveloped countries, became significant but did not strongly impact the American economy. Trade with Japan, on the other hand, in automobiles and high tech electronic equipment did have a major effect on the automobile and electronics industries. In the case of automobiles the Japanese had lower labor costs and produced an overall higher quality vehicle at competitive prices. In the case of electronics, particularly computers, the Japanese were able to raise the yield[1] rate of computer chips, and so could sell them at a lower cost than American computer chip makers.

The situation changed significantly in the 1990's when China was given "Most Favored Nation" status which reduced import duties on Chinese goods to the same as other countries

---

[1] Computer chips are made in batches like cookies. Only a percentage of the computer chips in a batch are free of defects. The percentage of defect free chips is the yield of the chip making process. The Japanese had succeeded in making high yield batches by refining the production techniques through repeated experimentation. They followed a similar process in developing the first ink jet printers.

with the lowest import duties. This seemingly modest change in import duties enabled the Chinese to successfully compete in American markets. China took full advantage of this boon and Chinese imports soared over succeeding years leading to a major trade imbalance in China's favor. As a result of the trade advantages of China, India and other countries America is slowly being impoverished. Tied to impoverishment is a declining standard of living, a diminished hope for the future, increasing crime (much of it surreptitious), a declining industrial and manufacturing base, and a growing sense of insecurity that is leading to social unrest and a feeling that a rigid class structure is developing in America – thus the suggestions of class warfare starting to appear in the media.

In this chapter we will propose a solution to the American trade imbalance based on the gradual imposition of a new tariff on imports based on the differential in average wages between the United States and its major trading partners.

The Problems Created by a Seriously Adverse Trade Imbalance

Tariffs (import duties) have been viewed as a hindrance to world trade, as a cause of economic inefficiencies, and as a cause of the Great Depression when large tariff barriers were rapidly put in place near the beginning of the Depression.

However tariffs have had major benefits in protecting fledgling industries in 19th century America, and similarly in other countries. If we look at the present-day American economy we see the following problems that largely result from the liberal US trade policies and particularly from the granting of Most Favored Nation status to China in the early 1990's:

1. A rapid decline in the US electronics, biomedical, manufacturing, and other industries resulting in unemployment, large social service costs (such as unemployment benefits), loss of worker pensions, and loss of workers' health insurance.
2. A generational break that is creating a generation of unskilled, uneducated, unemployed young people not psychologically motivated to work.
3. A decline in the US ability to gear up for a longer war of the type of WW II. The plants are closed that could be converted to weapons construction. For example, in WW II automobile assembly plants were rapidly converted to massive aircraft production. That capability no longer exists. The US is unable to fight a sustained war – especially since many parts for weaponry are imported from potential advisories.
4. The declining economy is causing major social problems: widespread despair of the future, social unrest and insecurity, a breakdown of hope in the future for children, and a separation into a polarizing class view of America: the "haves" and the "have not's."

The backdrop of these problems that results directly from the failure of American industry to compete with low wage countries, and their cartels, is a failed American tariff policy.

This failure is made more graphic by the realization that import duties were the main source of revenue for the US government for much of the 1800's.

A possible Solution Based on Creating a Tariff Structure Based on Wage Differentials between Countries

The fundamental source of our massive trade deficit is the wide disparity in wages between the US and developing countries such as China and India. While imports from these countries have the benefit of lower prices for consumers and we like to see an increase in the standard of living of these countries, the large size of the trade deficit, the drain on the American economy, the destruction of entire industries, and the consequent social ills such as unemployment make it necessary to level the playing field so that American made goods can compete with foreign exports in American markets without a decrease in the wages of American workers and their standard of living.

There is only one reasonable mechanism that can equalize the opportunity for American made goods to compete in the American marketplace: higher import duties. We propose the additional import duties be applied to major trading partners in Asia and Europe and that it be based on the difference in the average wage in each country with the American average wage. We further propose that the new duties be gradually increased from a proportion of the wage differences to fully account for the wage differences over a ten year period. The reason for a gradually increasing duty is to minimize economic disruptions that might occur if the full duty was imposed immediately. Foreign countries can adapt to the new duties in the ten year period. American industry can respond to the challenge by expanding and restarting industries in the ten year period knowing that they will be able to compete with low wage foreign competitors.

While the actual duty structure that would be imposed will probably be more complex, and might be different for different industries, we will now outline a duty structure that embodies these concepts (for one product item) and creates a level playing field for domestic and foreign workers.

The duty we propose for each major trading partner is:

1. Determine the average wage of American workers and of workers in each major trading partner.
2. For each country individually determine the difference between the average American labor cost for the item and the average foreign country labor cost of the item.
3. Divide the difference in labor costs by ten. This is the yearly increment in duty for the item.
4. After one year impose an additional duty (if the item had a previous duty) equal to the yearly increment in duty found in step 3.
5. In each following year up to the sixth year increase this duty by the yearly increment.
6. In the sixth year re-evaluate step 2 again for current labor cost differences and reset the yearly increment adding it year by year to the previous total duty increment.
7. When the total labor costs difference duty equals the difference between the American labor costs for an item and the foreign country's labor costs then the duty is not increased.

The above wage differential import duty specification is illustrated by the following example. We assume a product item is valued at $30 and the country of origin average labor cost for the item is

$15. Suppose the US labor cost would be $50. Then following the above seven steps we calculate the differential labor cost duty per item to be:

1. American labor cost = $50. Foreign labor cost = $15;
2. Difference in labor costs = $35.
3. Yearly increment in duty = $35/10 = $3.50.
4. Year two new duty = $3.50.
5. Year three through year six duties are: $7, $10.50, $14, $17.50 respectively per item.
6. Suppose Difference in labor costs is now $20 for the item in year 6. (Foreign wages rose.) Then the new yearly increment is $20/10 = $2 and the year 7 through year 11 duties are $19.50, $20, $20, $20, $20 respectively per item.

Thus the $20 labor cost differential in the last five years lead to a duty of $20 on a $30 item leading to an imported product total cost of $30 plus $15 (increased foreign labor cost) plus $20 = $65 compared to an American made cost of $65 if American wages do not increase and the cost of materials remains the same for the US and the foreign country[2] - equality.

In this way we can reduce or eliminate the impact of low foreign wages and give American industry and workers a chance to compete. To economists who feel this is a retrograde step in international trade and efficient world trade we reply that the need to help America maintain its standard of living is of more importance. American economic strength and a strong domestic

---

[2] Again we note that this simple approach will probably be modified with greater detail if implemented.

economy are required for a stable country and its defense – the major source of world peace at present.

The preceding process for imposing a labor cost differential duty can be generalized to the case of all products from a foreign country by taking the labor cost of each imported item, scaling it up to the US labor cost of the item by multiplying the foreign labor cost per item by the ratio of the US average cost of labor divided by the foreign country average cost of labor. This procedure generates a US labor cost per item. Then one can use steps 1 through 7 above to obtain a wage differential duty by country for each type of imported product.

Outsourcing Work to Foreign Countries

There has been a growing tendency to outsource various jobs to foreign countries such as telephone help services and telephone bill collection. This policy, which many US companies have been using, has several negative effects:

1. It eliminates entry level jobs for young adults. It has helped increase the pool of unemployed, mostly college educated young adults resulting in despair, inability to repay government guaranteed education loans, and increased welfare costs for many of the families of these young people.
2. It has deprived the US government of income tax revenues from what might have been young employed adults.
3. It has exasperated many people hoping to obtain information from help lines only to find the foreign

help line support teams often lack the necessary language skills and/or technical knowledge.

A solution for this problem is to regulate outsourcing to foreign countries by requiring an outsourcing license, and to impose an outsourcing tax payable by the outsourcing company equal to the difference between the comparable US labor costs of the work and the foreign cost of the work.

Again, to minimize the impact of the new tax it should be implemented gradually – perhaps 25% of the total wage difference in the first year, 50% of the difference in the second year, 75% in the third year and 100% in the fourth year and the years thereafter. Thus foreign countries and US companies will be able to adjust gradually to the changed circumstances.

The results will be a level playing field for young Americans and foreign workers, companies will be able to continue outsourcing overseas if they wish, a significant increase in US government income without raising individual income taxes, a lower outflow of US dollars, help for US young adults to repay college loans, and help to restore hope in the future for America's young adults.

Additional Cutbacks in the Outflow of US Dollars

While the imposition of wage differential duties will generate large revenues for the US government of the scale of tens of billions of dollars, action must be taken to further restrict the drain of dollars from the American economy by Foreign Aid and defense commitments abroad.

Current Foreign Aid payments should be given careful scrutiny to make sure that they are of benefit to the US and the people of the recipient foreign nations. It is well known that large amounts of US foreign aid are basically a bribe that winds up in the pockets of corrupt foreign officials. This type of abuse can no longer be tolerated.

The use of US forces in foreign trouble spots should only be allowed if it directly affects the safety of the United States or important foreign allies.

The war in Iraq while satisfying a perceived form of payback has not led to a safer America. It has resulted in many dead and severely injured Americans (Over 4,000 American soldiers died in Iraq.) that far outnumber the deaths in the World Trade Center disaster. Iraq is likely to revert to a Muslim extremist government after the US withdrawal. Thus the US does not derive a long term benefit from the Iraqi war despite massive costs (The Iraqi war that began in 2003 cost over an estimated one trillion dollars.) and many Americans killed and injured. The war in Afghanistan appears to be following a similar path with Muslim extremists poised to seize control after the projected American withdrawal. Afghani President Karzai anticipates this event and is clearly distancing himself from America.

Rather than fight countries with American soldiers in the manner of Iraq and Afghanistan, we should use drones, missiles and aircraft on carriers and on air bases to force prospective enemies to behave. Misbehavior would lead to air attacks to selectively destroy nuclear facilities, air bases, naval bases and army bases. One can visualize the impact on a foreign country if a massive number of low cost drones were launched from aircraft carriers - repeatedly for days and possibly weeks to bomb a hostile nation – as we did in round one with Iraq. The psychological impact of continuous bombardment would be enormous and would soon bring an adversary to the bargaining table to resolve issues with no loss of American life and relatively low costs during and after the conflict.

In a more general air war, massive disruption of a foreign enemy will likely lead to success for the US without heavy US casualties. Although some losses are likely in an air war they will be less than those in a ground war. The US would also not need to fund the rebuilding of a country as it is doing in Iraq.

The expenditures in the Iraqi and Afghani conflicts amounted to well over a trillion dollars of ill-spent dollars. Taking the life of Osama bin Laden was not worth the cost in American military lives and casualties.[3] He was effectively removed as a concern by the increased security measures in the US and elsewhere. Expensive revenge is not a smart move.

Benefits for America and Its Trading Partners

The proposed changes in import duties, and the introduction of an outsourcing tax to reflect relative labor costs with foreign countries, will have many benefits that could lead to a healthy economy and a federal budget without a deficit. Some of these benefits are:

1. It will gradually eliminate the inequity in competition with foreign countries with low wages.
2. The jobless rate of Americans will decline because they will now be able to compete successfully in the marketplace for goods and services.

---

[3] In fairness President Obama inherited this mission from the previous administration and it was supported by the vast majority of the American people.

3. New industries will start up; existing industries will be able to expand.
4. Tax revenues will increase as employment rises.
5. The federal government will derive hundreds of billions of dollars per year from the new import duties and the tax on foreign outsourcing.
6. The need to increase taxes or reduce government services to obtain a balanced federal budget will be eliminated.
7. The increase in jobs will lead to a reduction in welfare costs and unemployment benefits.
8. Companies will now be able to fund reasonable health insurance and pensions easing the burden of federal resources needed for these purposes.
9. The military industry will be able to find sources for its hardware within this country.
10. Medicines and vitamins will be produced in this country.
11. The danger to our aircraft companies of being underpriced by foreign competition will be eventually eliminated. This will benefit our balance of payments whose major export advantage is in the sale of large jets.
12. The new import duties will be somewhat like a Value Added Tax (VAT) for primarily imported goods without the overhead of collecting a VAT on every sale. Most European governments rely strongly on a VAT for revenue.
13. The import duties will stimulate growth in the domestic economy.
14. An important goal of the US is to stimulate a higher standard of living in foreign countries. A wage differential duty will make it easier for foreign countries to increase wages without losing their competitive low cost labor

advantage. Long term it will encourage rising living standards in foreign countries. Many of these countries are siphoning their income due to trade surpluses into their military rather than the people.

15. Retrieving lost jobs will raise the hope of a better future in America in young people.

Possible Problems Resulting from the Proposed Tariff Structure

Naturally, as in any change, there will be negatives associated with the change. In the present case we will see that the benefits far outweigh the problems.

Perhaps the major potential problem would be the immediate imposition of large new import duties and of a tax on foreign outsourcing. This potential problem is eliminated by a gradual imposition of these measures that will give America and foreign countries the time needed to gradually adapt to the changed trade conditions. Rapid drastic economic changes hurt people.

America will have time to expand existing industries to handle the increased volume of domestic business. Foreign countries will have time to adjust to a lowered American demand for their goods and services by developing an internal demand for their goods and services through a rise in wages and a consequent rise in their standard of living with an increased internal need for more goods and services.

We foresee the following problems due to higher import duties and a tax on foreign outsourcing:

1. Spot shortages might develop as American industries expand. This problem will be ameliorated by market forces that will increase prices if demand should exceed supplies – Capitalism at work.

2. Workers in affected foreign countries may resent this action of the US government. While this reaction is not something Americans would like, it is important to note they took American jobs and know how without showing any great concern for American workers. America is at least willing to bear the weight of this trade imbalance for ten more years as a humanitarian gesture. An understanding attitude from foreign governments coupled with the point that a bankrupt America will benefit nobody should make this problem short lived.

3. It is possible that American companies will not take advantage of this opportunity and grow their businesses. However, the hunger of the American people to overcome the present situation should lead to an increase in entrepreneurial spirit that can be stimulated by federal tax incentives and grants/loans.

4. There could be adverse political consequences in our relations with other nations. The gradualness of the increase of duties and taxes should make foreign governments more sympathetic to the American predicament and the need for an equable balance of payments. We discuss the particular cases of China and India in the next section.

5. Prices for goods in this country will rise. But a decline in unemployment will make price rises acceptable if its leads to a sharp decline in unemployment.

Thus we conclude the negatives of the proposed solution are far outweighed by the benefits. This plan of action puts America on the road to solvency.

Chinese and Indian Resistance?

Undoubtedly! Clearly, the overwhelming beneficiaries of the present situation are China and India. Both countries have grown enormously – primarily through funding from the deficit in the American balance of payments. The enormous outflow of US dollars has led America to the brink of a de facto bankruptcy both in government and at the level of the American people. Enormous numbers of people are barely making ends meet and often need to get loans from banks and relatives to pay bills.

Our proposal for import duties and taxes will be met with a negative reaction particularly from China and India. But they would prefer a solvent United States to a bankrupt US. No one wants their best customer to go bankrupt!

So our view is that they will acquiesce in the duties and tax realizing that they cannot extract money in large amounts from America indefinitely.

China

China has embarked on an aggressive trade and financial program which uses the following questionable methods:

1. Taking advantage of low wages for free workers together with reportedly large numbers of slave laborers to take a dominant position in world trade and particularly with the US.

2. China has engaged in robber baron practices and created cartels in important items such as rare earth metals as well as common consumer items such as vitamin C. In the case of vitamin C China sold it at a loss to drive competitors out of business and then achieved a monopoly in vitamin C. All vitamin C is now made in China. These tactics supported by a massive amount of cash have put competing industries in other countries at a severe disadvantage. Should the US ever engage in hostilities with China over, perhaps, Chinese expansion into oil rich Central Asia the US would be hard put to engage in a protracted war because of China's direct and indirect (via Japan and Korea) control of the production of computer chips and other electronic instruments. Recently it appears that the US Congress, to contain costs, decided to procure weapons from the lowest price source regardless of the country of origin. This blow to the US military commitment to support a domestic military armaments industry will have a disastrous effect in the future. The US has to some extent fallen within the "Chinese Coprosperity Sphere."

3. China has pursued a monetary policy designed to keep the value of its currency low in relation to the US dollar. This helps the Chinese keep export prices low

and constitutes another example of China's unfair trade practices.

What will China do if the US follows our import duty and outsourcing tax? It will probably do the following:

1. Unleash its North Korean "running dog" to make trouble for the US and South Korea short of actual warfare. A dead enemy is not a good customer.
2. It could cash in all or part of its trillion dollars of US bonds. Doing so would trash the US dollar and destroy the values of the dollars received from cashed bonds. It would also destroy China's ability to sell in the US for devalued dollars. Net result: China will not play this card.
3. It could impose duties on US goods sold to China. But, except for raw materials it needs, the imports of US goods is very little. Thus this tactic will not significantly harm the US.
4. China could go to war – an extreme measure. But this would decisively destroy the basis of their increasing prosperity.
5. It could embargo strategic goods needed by the US. But only rare earth metals are currently their only card and US companies are now developing alternate sources for rare earth metals.

We conclude that China will accept import duties grudgingly.

India

India has become a center for a massive help line, sales and telephone answering service industry, and, most importantly, a computer programming industry. These outsource industries work for US companies. They use workers with significantly lower wages to replace skilled, more highly paid US workers. The basis of India's success in these areas is a large pool of English speaking workers. Several hundred thousand US workers have lost their jobs due to outsourcing to India.

We propose to tax foreign outsourcing to make skilled American workers competitive with Indian workers, and skilled workers in other nations. By gradually imposing a tax on outsourced labor, US workers will be able to compete with Indian and other workers in these areas on the basis of skills not salaries.

India will undoubtedly protest this tax. But America will benefit by higher quality help lines, and the maintenance of skilled worker jobs – particularly computer programmers.

US competency in vital computer programming skills will be maintained so that the US will have a domestic source of these skills should the need arise. Since this tax will be gradually implemented Indian workers can readjust their careers in the rapidly expanding Indian economy. Since the tax leads to cost of labor equality, Indian workers are not excluded from working for US companies if they have a skill set that an American company needs. The tax merely levels the playing field in salaries.

How long can China Play its North Korean Card?

North Korea exists because of its support by China. North Korea would crumble without Chinese economic and military aid, and the implied threat to help North Korea if attacked by South Korea or the United States.

North Korea has started threatening the United States and South Korea with a nuclear pre-emptive first strike. They could not do this without implicit, private Chinese agreement and, perhaps, encouragement.

The United States is China's best customer by far. Privately the US is probably "gently" reminding China about the mistake of hurting its customers.

It is time for the US to make a bold <u>public</u> policy statement that China would be denied entry to the US market if North Korea starts hostilities. Then the North Korean paper tiger will show its lack of teeth.

2. A Destabilized America

Once upon a time there was a country with workers who generally earned decent salaries, who had job security, who had health insurance paid for by their employer, and who could look forward to a secure retirement with a livable pension plus a Social Security pension. Government workers in this country generally received slightly lower pay but had strong job security, health insurance, and a livable pension after perhaps twenty years of service. The mail service was decent and had a more or less balanced budget. Spouses did not have to work to meet living expenses and children had the benefit of an at home parent.

This mythical country was the United States of the 1950's and 1960's. Since then the United States has developed into a seemingly much wealthier nation, secure in its leadership of much of the world, and without the nuclear threat of the Cold War. But it has also developed a serious social instability due to many causes. This instability has not become very visible as yet. It is cloaked by financial and social band aids, and by the multitude of minor issues, seemingly unrelated, that reflect a general unrest and dissatisfaction with the condition of the nation. The media and political leaders are generally unwilling to put the pieces of the events in the country together to see the general destabilization of the country that exists in the minds of the people and that only reveals itself in violent incidents and in events that reflect a general insecurity about the future.

The litany of worries of the American people can be summarized as a general concern about every aspect of their lives and the future of the country. We now turn to consider the state of the nation at present and in the foreseeable future.

Instability in the Lives of the People

The decline of American industries such as the automobile industry, the computer industry and the aircraft industry has changed the job climate for American workers. Company pensions have been largely eliminated; company health insurance has become less comprehensive. Workers are more or less forced to take buyouts to leave their employers. Even companies with a legendary employee loyalty such as IBM have succumbed to buyouts of older workers.

Wall Street has worsened the situation by usually rewarding companies for discarding employees and thus lowering expenses. Many companies with declining revenues lay off workers or "buy out" employees into retirement to lower expenses in such a way as to have a larger "bottom line." Higher profits are at the expense of employees' job security.

The consequence of this loss of industrial strength, whose basis is generally in the transfer of jobs overseas, is stress for those who retain their jobs, and for people who may have joined a company expecting a lifetime of employment and who, then, were forced into unemployment and in many cases despair.

The middle class has been driven to a level of uncertainty not seen since the Great Depression. Poverty and bare bones living have become widespread with America's twenty-four million unemployed, and countless underemployed, workers leading the way. Despairing young people often turn to drugs and homelessness. The bulk of these people are not seen because of help from relatives and friends.

And most importantly a college education is no longer an entry point for a good job.

For the first time since the 1930's people talk of a class war due to the hardening of class lines – upward mobility, the hope of WW II veterans in the 1950's, is not probable in the view of the majority of lower Middle Class Americans. And so the hope for a future better life for themselves and their children is seriously diminished. With the loss of hope, crime based on theft and violence has increased. Much of this increase is not apparent in crime statistics for several reasons. Among the reasons people underreport crime are: fear of retaliation, subtle crimes where small amounts or items of small value are stolen with which police are unable to cope due to lack of manpower, and the fear of criminal gangs.

The net result is an American people, which is far more insecure and anxious than at any time in the past fifty years. Job insecurity. Unemployment insecurity. Financial insecurity. Personal safety insecurity. Crime insecurity. Evidence of these issues is the almost weekly murder sprees of disturbed individuals. Yes, easy gun ownership provides disturbed individuals with weapons. But the root cause of many violent multiple murders are loss of jobs and/or a despair of the future. Secure people with stable jobs do not often engage in murder or crime.

The current psychological state of the people is a major threat to the future stability of America.

Instability in Government

A good government should be a source of stability for a nation. But a good government can develop problems through unwise policies. We saw an example of an unwise policy in chapter 1 when we considered the impact of lowering trade barriers for countries with a low wage structure. Such countries can out compete the US in its own markets, and cause the economic structure of the country, and the standard of living of its people, to decline.

The increasing, multi-decade decline in the US trade balance has led America to a disastrous financial condition. In addition it has jeopardized the country's security: we couldn't gear up production for another world war since we are now without a large industrial base to convert to defense production.

Recently it has become apparent that the US government is becoming increasingly polarized. Republicans and Democrats have been unable to unite behind a program to balance the federal budget. They vigorously differ on how to increase taxes and how to reduce expenditures. As a result the government is in a precarious position due to a failure to negotiate compromises. Without a successful solution to the budget impasse the country's future is uncertain.[4] The eventual results range from a severe economic contraction to a drift in direction that is dangerous from a long term viewpoint to a solution with which nobody is happy.[5]

A major source of governmental uncertainty and possible instability is the ever increasing federal debt. It is pretty clear that

---

[4] In the past few days a budget compromise has been reached. March 31, 2013.
[5] Probable result of the compromise budget.

much of this debt cannot be paid off.[6] Since it is very likely to increase substantially in the next ten years the value of the US dollar, and investments in stock and bonds that depend on the dollar, are becoming suspect. The specter of large inflation also looms on the current horizon.

These economic uncertainties are of great concern to Americans as well as foreigners. It has led people to invest heavily in gold, other precious metals, and in the Swiss franc. More than anything this governmentally inspired instability disturbs the American people and the future of the republic.

Part of governmental instability is the insecurity of government employees. These people became government employees knowing that they would not be paid as well as those in the private sector. But they expected, that if they performed their duties properly, they would have secure lifetime employment and a good pension. Both of these expectations are no longer the case. Postal workers exemplify the change with forced retirements and layoffs. The US mail has suffered as a result. For example, there is an increased rate of pilferage by postal workers who know that they will be dismissed.

Other US agency personnel are also feeling the stress of government cutbacks. Their morale and the performance of their duties is in jeopardy. This problem is particularly acute for the US military where cutbacks are almost certain. The ability of the US to defend itself in the future is an open question.

---

[6] There is good reason for the debt not to be erased completely as it offers a mechanism for secure investments for individuals, financial institutions and business. However the magnitude of the debt should probably be reduced since it jeopardizes the value of the US dollar.

Instability of the Future America

Looking ahead to the next fifty years of America we see a country that is beset with an enormous number of issues that might lead to radical changes in the nature of the government and in the lives of the people.

First there are the economic problems that might undermine the welfare of the people by eroding salaries, savings, and pensions. The response of the people might lead to the type of insurrections that America experienced in the 19th century in various parts of the country. People will strongly respond to a challenge to their families' well-being.

The primary economic problems that one can anticipate are ever widening federal and state debt, large surges of inflation wiping out the income and savings of the people, a decline in small business growth due to large company monopolization of the consumer marketplace, the development of large permanently unemployed, and of large permanently homeless, parts of society with no stake in society, and the extinction of the work ethic – a return to Victorian times.

Increasing Demands for Support from the People

The federal and state governments are faced with increasing demands for services and support from the American people. There is a feeling of entitlement which is the subject of increasing comment. Young people tend to want a clean well-paying job and tend to back away from the useful work such as plumbing, construction work, electrical work, and other occupations. Parents tend to want their children to go to college, obtain well-paying desk jobs, and "live happily ever after." Recreations are viewed as of equal importance with work. The net result is a country that is drifting towards a "bread and circuses" attitude that is troublesome in view of the strong work ethic of other countries in Europe and Asia.

Higher Small Business Barriers

Another problem that is important, but normally unremarked, is the decline of many categories of small business due to the onslaught of large businesses. Examples abound: the elimination of small hardware stores by hardware superstores, the decline of small fast food hamburger joints due to massive marketing and cost saving gimmicks such as poor quality meats by the large fast food chains, the elimination of small clothes stores and the corner drug stores by large chains of stores and so on. The cost of a small business startup is also growing rapidly due to necessary high advertising costs and high construction and furnishing costs. The result is an increasingly high barrier to small business creation which is known to be a major source of employment. Employment growth will be adversely impacted and a new generation of entrepreneurs will face increasing hurdles.

"Bread and Circuses" America?

Many commentators have compared the US to Imperial Rome. Like Rome where the small farms that furnished the Roman government with great leaders and the Roman legions with strong soldiers, the United States is rapidly creating a large "entity" economy: large businesses, large agri-business, and large government. The trend to a large number of government dependents through welfare, Social Security, and medical insurance as well as other services, is comparable to the Roman drift towards decay.

Growth of Corruption

The US has prided itself as a country with much less governmental corruption than other countries. This view is becoming less and less correct as the Congress, and state and local governments as well as law enforcement personnel, and judges, up to the level of the Secret Service become more and more corrupted by criminal organizations and increasingly by Mexican, and Central and South American, drug cartels. It has been remarked that very few senators leave office as the same financial level as when they were elected. The American public is becoming increasingly cynical of political leaders and government in general.

At some point, if this trend continues, the American people will face either governmental tyranny or massive civil unrest.

To make matters worse the corruption and criminal conduct of members of the government is being transmitted to the people leading society to widespread cheating, theft and other criminal conduct. This trend portends a society without the trust and cooperation that makes democracy work. We then become a ruthless, greedy, stressed, anxiety ridden society unworthy of our heritage from the nation's founding fathers.

US Trend to a Third World Raw Materials Economy

The decline of major industries in the US has left us with a consumption oriented society without the resources to support our spending. One area in which the US is doing relatively well is raw material production: coal, natural gas, metals and agricultural products.

This trend towards a mining and agricultural economy is reminiscent of many third world countries and can be viewed as US progress towards 3rd world status. If this is the state of the American economy in the future then it is clear the prosperity of this country will end as well as the American Dream.

Population Trends

A related, disquieting trend is the growing population. Today the population is about 300,000,000. In a hundred years if the population trend continues we will very likely have a population of at least a billion and perhaps much more. Then we will have followed in the footsteps of India – a rich country of 300,000,000 in 1850 and a poor country of a billion plus inhabitants from the 1950's. Clearly it is time to consider population trends seriously if we wish to have a prosperous future America for our descendants.

Hope for America!

Mr. Peter Lynch, noted sock analyst, is reputed to once have remarked, "Whenever a stock reaches a point where I can only hope it improves, the stock usually turns out to be a loser."

This author believes that, while America is currently at low ebb, there is every hope for its recovery if wise policies are pursued.

We think the issues raised in this rather somber chapter can be resolved by a dedicated, aroused American people who lead their political leaders to make the right choices for our future. The remainder of this book is dedicated to advocating policies that can lead to a bright future that continues the American Dream.

3. Social Security, Medicare, and Obamacare

These three topics are grouped together because the vast majority of Americans believe they are essential to their welfare under current, and probably future, economic conditions. Obamacare is perhaps the least well-defined and least appreciated by Americans but it can, if wisely implemented, be a great help to an important segment of the American people: younger people.

The most important purpose of all three programs is the welfare of the people. Social Security and Medicare are intended to thank older people who have worked for a lifetime to make America great.

Social Security

Social Security is a fair but not overly generous program. One piece of evidence of its nature is a statement made to me by the CEO of a major food company that numbers dog food among its many products. Rather embarrassingly, in a low voice, he said, "We are getting requests from old people on Social Security for recipes for dog food." These requests show that Social Security provides a sustenance level of support at best. Seeing oldsters packing grocery bags in food stores buttresses this point.

Another reason supporting the need for Social Security is the blatant age discrimination in jobs throughout the economy. Oldsters are usually unable to get decent jobs unless they own the company – something very few oldsters do. Most jobs have retirement dates that nowadays are enforced regardless of the quality of an employees work or the employees past contributions to the company. In addition a common business practice is to offer older, more highly paid workers a buyout and replace them with lower paid younger workers. Often the buyout offer comes with a veiled threat of a layoff in the near future if the worker declines the buyout offer.

A rather blatant case of age discrimination that I observed was the termination of the employment of a publishing company executive who created the mainstay product of the company. The product bears his name.

Should we increase Social Security payments? – Not possible with the state of the Federal budget deficit and the Social Security System's available funds. Should we eliminate or severely reduce Social Security payments? No. For several reasons including simple humanity, it is a long standing commitment made by the government on which it should not renege. Also oldsters buy things with their payments contributing to the economy. Cutting back on Social Security will lower economic conditions. Thus a reduction of Social Security payments will be injurious to America – both financially and psychologically.

Medicare

Medicare is under strong attack as a possible area where a reduction is possible to help lower the Federal Budget deficit. There is no doubt that Medicare is a humane way of helping oldsters in need of health care – people who built and defended the country. They deserve decent health care – although with steadily rising health care costs they cannot afford it.

Changing the Medicare rules is the proposed solution to reducing Medicare costs. However reductions in doctors' and hospital fees which are low compared to non-Medicare fees, will only lead to their tacit or explicit defection from the Medicare system.

As it is, many older people are confused by Medicare rules and the way Medicare is administered. They seek health care not knowing if they have coverage or not because of arbitrary decisions by the staff of Medicare Advantage and Medicare Supplement programs that are supposed to lower the copay that Medicare often requires.

Ways of Reducing Medicare Outlays Gracefully

We need a graceful solution to the Medicare expense issue given the social need for Medicare which the overwhelming majority of older citizens expect and need, given the recognition of the impact on the Federal deficit, and given a desire for a humane solution.

There appear to be several ways of humanely reducing Medicare costs. These ways are based on the premise that life is worth continuing if a person is aware of their surroundings and does not have total dementia or Alzheimer's disease. They also are based on the premise of a death with dignity – not attempting to prolong life for terminally ill patients. Thirdly they are based on the need to prevent abuse of Medicare with unnecessary procedures, medicine or operations. With these thoughts in mind we suggest the following guiding Medicare principles:

1. A committee composed solely of doctors will review any proposed surgery or procedure costing over $1,000.

2. Doctors and hospitals will be limited each year to not increasing any Medicare costs by more than the increase in the Cost of Living Index.
3. Terminally ill patients will be covered by Medicare for pain killing medication only and, if the patient is in a nursing facility, the continuation of the appropriate support from Medicare.
4. Patients that are totally out of contact with reality due to dementia or other diseases will only receive medication for pain and, if the patient is in a nursing facility, the continuation of the appropriate support from Medicare.

The author has seen the deplorable conditions in nursing homes – not due to lack of care – but due to total loss of contact with reality: patients crowding their wheel chairs around nurse stations with blank stares on their faces. Item 4 above reflects the meaninglessness of life under these conditions and the view that subjecting these patients to life prolonging procedures and operations is not to the patient's advantage or to society's advantage.

We believe the above proposals will slow the growth in Medicare costs significantly – not for selfish reasons but to enable funding of socially more beneficial needs such as Obamacare.

A further method of reducing Medicare costs, which requires an emphasis on more medical research, is to develop medicines, procedures, and genetic engineering to substantially lower the maladies and diseases of old age. A healthier older generation will of itself lower Medicare costs. The goal is not to extend life but to make life worth living into old age. The beginning wave of aged baby boomers is a strong motivation for this research and for the above stated four methods of directly lowering Medicare costs.

Some will feel that there is a coldness in implementing these proposals. The author invites those persons to visit health care facilities with a large number of older patients and ask if themselves if they still think a life without a mind is worth living.

Obamacare

We use the term Obamacare to signify the general concept put forward by the President to provide health insurance to those young people, not eligible for Medicare, who are unable to obtain health insurance at an affordable price. We would augment the Obamacare concept with a proposal for home health care provided to all children below 6 years of age.

The purpose of a government medical insurance program is to maintain the health of the people who otherwise might not be able to pay their health care costs. There are two reasons why we should have such a program: a desire to have humane treatment of the less fortunate, and the need to have a healthy citizenry to work and, if necessary, to defend the country.

President Obama has proposed a program to insure people below Medicare age (65) who are unable to obtain health insurance because of low income or health risk. This program will be funded by money taken from Medicare which, in turn, will reduce expenses by changing Medicare rules.

While Obamacare might solve a major social problem: inadequate health insurance for the "uninsurable" it appears to be a misstep in terms of meeting the goal stated in the second paragraph of this section. The social problems that it does not address are revealed in the news almost every week: child abuse and maltreatment, mental problems of mothers (and fathers), mental/behavioral problems of criminals stemming from bad childhoods, and mass killings of people by psychotic (typically unemployed) individuals. While we cannot escape from the problems of the human condition, we can hope to alleviate these problems by good care for children and meaningful employment for adults.

Consequently we propose that Obamacare be replaced by a more comprehensive program which will initially result in a larger federal deficit but will eventually result in lower federal and state expenditures to remedy the problems mentioned above. Our first suggestion is to replace Obamacare with an extension of Medicare to birth. The first benefit of this extension will be a cost savings due to eliminating the need for a separate duplicate bureaucracy implicit in Obamacare. The specifics of this proposed extension are:

1. Medicare will be extended to all citizens and legal immigrants except those covered by a private health care insurance, those having high incomes (perhaps greater than $250,000), and those having large wealth (greater than $2,000,000? excepting the value of their home).
2. Children under six years of age will have extended care using a corps of visiting nurses who will visit the children's homes, give routine examinations, check the parents' condition, advise parents on child care, and call in a doctor or counselor if necessary. Nurses will bring endangered children to the attention of the authorities for remedial

action BEFORE child abuse.[7] Nurse visits will take place every six months after a child's birth.

3. Companies that have health insurance programs for their employees will be required to use their plan benefits before employees use Medicare benefits.

4. Companies without (or terminating) comprehensive employee health insurance will have to pay a higher payroll tax (determined by Congress) with the increment reflecting the average cost of Medicare for the company's employees.

The purpose of the proposed extension of Medicare and the supplemental child care provision for home visits by nurses for children under six, is to promote the general welfare of the people and, particularly, to ensure that children get a good start in life. Due to divorces and disjointed life styles, many of today's parents lack knowledge of basic parenting skills that nurse visits can help rectify. This problem leads to abused children who then grow into maladjusted adults who fill prisons and engage in crime and murder. To the extent that we can, we should try to give children a healthy, safe home atmosphere and reduce the problems that now plague our society.

Since people over 65 years of age are a large fraction of the US population and likely to grow larger, and since young people have on average much less health problems, the cost of the proposed extension of Medicare to all will not be as significant as one might naively expect.

---

[7] It is not uncommon to read about serious child abuse and death due to disturbed parents in the news.

Economic Benefit of Medicare, Social Security, and Federal Employment

Americans benefit from Social Security and Medicare. They also benefit from the large group of Federal employees. Individuals proposing cutbacks in these areas seem to have forgotten the benefits of these federal expenditures in their attempts to balance the federal budget through cutbacks and job terminations.

The large number of individuals benefiting from these programs, and Federal jobs, directly help the American economy by their spending and significantly smooth over the extremes of economic downturns. Economic downturns are a normal part of the economic cycle.

Federal spending helps stabilize the economy and provides a cushion for major downturns. Consequently, cutting back programs and terminating federal employment during a downturn, such as the one we are currently experiencing, accentuates an economic downturn and is counterproductive.

4. Education

Everybody is in favor of providing a good education to the nation's youth. Our political leaders all favor a good education. They often say that improving education will lead to more jobs, more skilled workers and a better life for all. Of course, the nice part of these assertions is that they serve to excuse solving current problems now and put the solution into the future. However America's youth and their parents know very well that the solution for the country's major problems: unemployment, declining industries, and poor economic conditions is not in education but rather in changes in current policies such as those advocated in this book – particularly in chapter 1.

Certain facts must furnish the basis for a sound education policy:

1. Not everyone can be a good student. Some students are not suited for education beyond the basic level due to intelligence levels, family atmosphere, and bad character. Throwing money at their further education is a mistake.
2. Not everyone should go to college. The country needs blue collar workers as much as white collar workers. Young people who do not want a college education should not be forced through social or parental pressure to attend college. Indeed, many major figures such as Andrew Carnegie and Bill Gates either did not attend college or left college before graduation.

3. Education is a privilege for good people. Young people who are known juvenile delinquents should not be allowed to attend schools at the country's expense. They hurt the educational process for well-behaved young people and also waste money that could be better spent on the well-behaved students who want an education.

4. Not everyone is entitled to, or can have, a white collar job. Some young people will be happier in the skilled craft jobs or as labor. As a youth this author worked for a while for his town's highway department: collected garbage, worked on road maintenance, and did general work for his town. I noticed the regular employees of the highway department were a mixed crew of Americans including an Indian from Oklahoma. Our boss – a former Marine sergeant had served in WW II. The one thing they had in common was security in their job and a certain sort of happiness – they knew they were doing something worthwhile that they could do well. When I was a white collar executive in major corporations I did not see the same level of contentment in most of my colleagues. Nor did I see general contentment in faculties when I was in academic life. Quite simply people should choose occupations that they can handle, that promote the general welfare of the country (even in a small way), and that give them security and contentment.

5. Rewarding teachers for giving high marks to students is a mistake. Teachers have often marked students on a curve in tough courses. But the excesses stemming from giving bonuses to teachers who give high grades to their students is fraught with difficulties. In a nearby high school I

understand that about 97% of the graduating seniors had A averages. Many other high schools have similar situations making it difficult for colleges and universities to select students for admission. Almost everybody who works wishes they had higher salaries. Salary increases in these times are not very common — particularly in hard pressed education budgets. So for the federal government to give bonuses to teachers for high student grades is a very flawed approach and should be ended.

How can We Improve Education?

At The School Level

At the level of the individual schools, public education must be viewed as a privilege funded by taxpayers — taxpayers who are often hard pressed financially. Thus we advocate a change from universal education without qualification to universal education *for those students who want it and will work at their studies.* From ninth grade onward through high school students who seriously misbehave or who clearly do not want to have a high school education should be exited.

This policy will free money to be used on serious students and remove a major discipline problem confronting the nation's schools.

I have noticed that some of the high school teachers of my acquaintance, who teach in inner city schools and in suburban schools, talk very loudly with obviously strained voices in social situations such as parties. The reason: they have to shout most of the time to be heard by their students who chatter away, ignoring the teacher's instruction.

Lastly, in view of increasing major violence at the nation's schools, each elementary and high school should have a detector and guard at its entrance to find students entering with guns, knives, or other weapons. Any student of any age found trying to enter with a weapon should be immediately dismissed permanently. Such students have many private school systems available should they wish to obtain to have a second chance at an education.

At the National Level

The federal teacher bonus program should be changed to give bonuses to teachers based on the performance of their students on a National Achievement Test created and managed by the federal government. A National Achievement test will eliminate the pressure on teachers to give high grades but will encourage them to teach well.

The National Achievement Test that we propose should have at least the following features:

1. It should be for high school seniors only in November so it could be available to colleges and universities at the student's request. November has few National holidays.
2. It should be administered at a location different from the schools by administrators not connected with the schools of the students being tested at that location.
3. It should be a comprehensive test of all subjects (except[8] Music and Art) and should last for 2 – 3 days.

---

[8] Reason: many disadvantaged youngsters are not familiar with these subjects at home and most schools do not offer Art or Music History or Appreciation courses.

4. The test should have questions in each subject area ranging from "easy" to "difficult" to clearly differentiate between students' performance so that a teacher bonus program can clearly identify schools that have done well by their students. It also should lead to a full four year college scholarship for the 100 highest performing students in the country.

5. The bonus system for teachers will be calculated from the test scores of the seniors. One simple way to determine bonuses which we feel should go to all levels of teachers from kindergarten through high school is:

   a. For each school system in the country determine the average of the test scores of the system's seniors taking the test.

   b. Set up a scale of bonus amounts per teacher based on the average of the system's seniors' scores. Higher average scores results in higher per teacher bonuses.

   c. Each school system will receive a bonus sum equal to the bonus per teacher times the total number of the teachers in the school system. The school system will decide on the specific bonus for each teacher from K though 12 in an equable way.

   d. The scale of bonuses will be set up in such a way that when combined with the number of teachers in each system and totaled, the resulting total will equal the available federal budget appropriation. (This calculation can be done with a computer program.)

   e. The 100 top scored students taking the test each year will receive a full college scholarship covering tuition, and room and board together with travel money (to and from school) and a reasonable monthly allowance. They will be designated as Presidential Scholars and honored in a White House ceremony.

The bonus program that we have suggested will result in a fair program that will encourage teachers at all levels to work together to produce better educated students.

5. Immigration

Immigration into a country has several purposes:

1. To populate an unfilled or sparsely filled country.
2. To provide cheaper labor than currently available in the country.
3. To provide a country with the needed skills that immigrants can provide.

The United States today is a populated country with its 300,000,000 plus million people. This population occupies much of the habitable land. The remaining land is desert land, mountains, necessary forest land and necessary farm land. The size of the population has led to a large water problem – the population of some areas needs potable water in excess of the available water. These problems have been mitigated by the transport of water from remote sources by aqueducts. Some examples are New York City and much of southern California. Given these circumstances and the massive waste disposal problems we now face due to a large population it is clear that the first purpose stated above no longer holds for the US. *The US has enough inhabitants.*

The second purpose is also questionable given the 24,000,000 unemployed and the, perhaps, 20,000,000 underemployed in the country. Bringing in cheap foreign labor reduces the chances of these people to find employment and lowers wages. In union parlance these immigrants are "scabs" that lower wages of American workers. Thus the apparent desire of Hispanic Americans in particular to open the doors wider to immigration, if realized, would actually harm their economic well-being. The second purpose is contrary to the well-being of all Americans. It was used in the 19th century by industrialists to keep workers' salaries low.

The third purpose has merit still. Bringing in workers with scarce skills such as medical people and scientists is good for the US. But it is not good usually for the countries that are deprived of their services.

With these points in mind we think it is reasonable to end immigration into the US except for workers with needed skills. In making this (controversial) statement we think of the future of the United States. It has 300,000,000 people now and is likely to have about a billion people in 100 years.[9] The growth to a billion inhabitants would profoundly change America and deepen the water and environmental problems that we now have. It is also likely to widen the gulf between the "haves" and "have nots" that is beginning to be a topic of discussion. Consider India which had a population of approximately 300,000,000 in 1850. At that time India was a rich country. It later became the "crown jewel" of the British Empire under Prime Minister Disraeli. One hundred years later India had a billion people consisting of a small minority of well off people and a very large number of poor people. Similar statements could be made about China and Indonesia.

In a sense America is now at a point corresponding to India in 1850. Now is the time to make decisions that will affect the

---

[9] The US population has approximately tripled in the previous 100 years.

future of the country. These decisions hinge critically on population growth. And population growth is strongly affected by the level of immigration. (Historically immigrants have tended to have larger families than native born Americans.) Thus we favor a graceful end to immigration by closing the application process now and admitting only those currently on waiting lists to enter.

As is currently the practice, Congress should be able to pass bills admitting people in specific job categories and specific individuals for good reason. Spouses, children and parents of US citizens and legal immigrants should also be allowed to take up residence in the country for humanitarian reasons.

The Question of Illegal Immigrants

America apparently has approximately eleven million illegal immigrants from a variety of countries. The expulsion of such a large number of people is neither practical nor is it desirable. Our political leaders of both parties recognize this.

The question before the US is now what to do with illegals. A number of solutions have been proposed. We propose what we believe is a fair and equable solution recognizing the courage and hardship required for their entry. They earned entry by the kind of effort and daring that we would like to see in all Americans.

Therefore we propose:

1. All illegal immigrants, who are employed, be given resident status, work permits and access to the same governmental and other services as native born Americans for a probationary period of ten years from the date of registering with the federal immigration authorities. Unemployed illegal immigrants will be sent back to their

home countries. If they return again then they will be sentenced to two years duty in a labor camp described below. After the two years duty they will be returned to their home country. If they return yet again then they will have to perform five years duty before being sent home.

2.   All illegal immigrants who commit a felony crime, and are convicted in court, in the ten year probationary period will serve the sentence specified by the court followed by two years of duty in labor camps set up to build fences and barricades, and/or to do environmental work, along the country's border. At the end of this time they will be paid a sum ($500?) and sent back to their home country. If they return again then they will serve five years in a labor camp and be sent back to their home country without pay.

3.   After the ten year probationary period without crime they will be allowed to become citizens through the standard citizenship process.

The labor camps would be set up by the US military, Border patrol and environmental agencies to perform work on border fences and environmental projects. Inmates would be adequately housed and fed and allowed to have visits from friends and families, who are legal residents of the US, consistent with their work schedule.

We believe this approach is fair and resolves the major problem associated with illegals – their possible criminal activity.

Preventing New Illegal Immigration

Unfortunately there will still be new illegals attempting to enter the country. We suggest this situation be handled in the following way:

1. Stringent border control will continue and be strengthened.
2. New Illegals who are caught will serve two years of duty in labor camps set up to build fences and barricades, and/or to do environmental work, along the country's border. At the end of this time they will be paid a sum ($500?) and sent back to their home country. If they return again then they will serve five years in a labor camp and be sent back to their home country without pay. Further returns would result in ten year labor camp sentences for each occurrence.
3. The US and Mexico will set up joint patrols to a distance of 50 miles on both sides of the border to apprehend illegals in transit and to fight the drug traffic. (Mexico is hard pressed to contain drug cartels operating inside its borders.)[10]

---

[10] A somewhat forgotten part of American history is the Mexican campaign of General 'Black Jack' Pershing before World War I when a weak Mexican central government was unable to prevent war lords such as Pancho Villa and other banditos from raiding Texas. Pershing, who later led the American Expeditionary Force sent to France, successfully ended their threat. Today when the Mexican government is hard pressed to defeat drug cartels and worried about reprisals to their troops and their families from a very vicious set of foes, joint patrols with the US Army may well be welcomed.

A personal anecdote about Pancho Villa and the type of character of the banditos in general is the experience of my wife's family in Mexico. My wife's great grandparents emigrated from the US to Mexico in the late 1800's and built a million acre empire of land, railroads and silver mines. Pancho Villa expropriated their property when he came to power. In addition he placed my wife's grandfather at age 14 in front of a firing squad who took aim at the youngster and then burst out laughing – not amusing to him as you might imagine. Then they ordered him and his family out of the country telling them never to return to Mexico. They did not; .Instead her grandfather went to California and eventually built an oil company. (Pancho Villa is currently very much out of favor with the Mexican government and people.) This anecdote illustrates both the savagery and the deep kindness of the Mexican people.

4. Employers hiring the new illegal immigrants will receive heavy fines and possible jail sentences.

A procedure with labor camp punishment similar to the above is necessary to avoid an endless cycle of repeated border crossings.

6. Media Excesses

The greatness of nations often has its beginning in groups of people with a unifying identity and a strong moral code. The decay of nations is often marked by a decline of unity and a decline in moral values. The United States was founded by groups of English colonists who for the most part shared a common identity and a common strong moral code.

As America developed the identity and moral code of the nation was still commonly held – the melting pot for immigrants worked.

In the past fifty years there has been a divergence in these commonly held beliefs due to the development of a "youth culture" that purposely deviated from the cultural values of their parents and often rejected the transfer of ideas and behavior that was the hallmark of earlier generations of Americans.

A large part of this new phenomenon "youth culture" was the development of new media – moving pictures, radio, television, the Internet, and other primarily electronic media.

The consequences of these changes are a breakdown in public morality, increasing violence, a breakdown in the American work ethic in favor of a feeling of entitlement, an increase in corruption and its acceptance as "natural", and an increase in violence that is increasingly based on a flood of illegal drugs into the country.

America today is a fragmented country with the only unifying feature that the federal government should solve all problems and provide for the people – a view which is diametrically opposite to that of generations before World War II.

The source of this change is primarily in the media which promotes sex, violence, easy living at the expense of parents and others, and a lack of guilt for the unfortunate consequences of one's actions. "Immorality and violence are cool."

We need a reversal of this trend if America is to survive as a free and prosperous nation. The nations that are currently doing well such as Japan and China have a unifying identity and a moral code that might differ from ours but serves to create a nation with a rectitude in the actions of their people.

How shall we change course as a nation? – by revamping the media to strengthen the fiber of the American people. In this chapter we suggest necessary changes in the media. The changes are not a breach of freedom of speech and of the press. These freedoms were designed to protect the discussion of political issues particularly with respect to government policy, taxes, and tariffs. They were not meant to protect the constant portrayal of crime, violence, and sexual excesses; and the overly extensive and invasive coverage of disasters. We now examine possible rules to reduce the media trend to public preoccupation with sex, violence, and excesses of the sort seen in the ancient Roman coliseums.

Television

Television has been transformed from a medium that portrayed the everyday life of generally moral Americans to the portrayal of the life styles of marginal groups in society with an emphasis on the weirdness and peculiarities of individuals whether it is nerds, "dweebs," Hollywood party wives, or reality races/shows with strange aspects. For example, in the past week a reality show displayed a "race" that included attending Vietnamese patriotic events such as dances, and exhibits of American bombers shot down during the Vietnamese war. One wonders at the insensitivity of television producers in such a case where so many American lives were lost and destroyed.

The large number of programs featuring non-traditional themes is also an issue. The number of such programs is very disproportionate to the percentage of the population that are "different." They result in a distorted view of American society where traditional families are still the norm. They make it difficult for parents trying to raise their children with traditional values. Where are the shows of the type of yesteryear such as "Lucy", "Father Knows Best" and so on that correspond to the life styles of most American families?

Television also glorifies crime and disasters by far more extensive coverage than they should have. It encourages copycat crimes – we now seem to have a massacre every week. It magnifies the concern over natural events such as earthquakes and glories in portrayals of the disastrous consequences with on the scene reports and interviews with victims.

Crime reporting makes a sort of hero out of criminals. Extensive publicity and celebrity appearances lead some people to crime as a way to get on TV. It also legitimizes criminal conduct to some extent – "lots of people are doing it."

These issues and the many more that could be raised (such as limits on news coverage of crime and violence, an end to selective extreme coverage of "newsworthy" figures, and an end coverage of criminal trials on TV) suggest that there should be a code of conduct with respect to TV programs and a federal government board to see that the code is enforced with substantial fines for misconduct as well as the possible loss of broadcasting rights for programs and stations.

Movies

The above comments apply to movies as well and a similar board should be created. Hollywood is an unreal part of Lalaland that has only a partial grasp of the needs and realities of the American people. It has led the country to a disastrous decline in public morality through its glorification of sex and violence – "After all that is how to sell a movie."

Those who might consider these suggestions as undemocratic should consider that the United Kingdom has had such a board without an abridgement of civil liberties or undue constraint on artistic freedom of expression.

Other Media

The Internet has similar defects as well. But with so many choices of web sites the effect on the nation's morality and integrity is somewhat lessened. By its nature it cannot be controlled by a governing board except on a world-wide basis although some countries such as China do censor web sites.

Picture taking cell phones and similar gadgets are open to abuse but they should be regulated by individuals and by the choice of companions who will not abuse their capabilities.

The Blurred Line between Reality and the Media

The portrayal of events on the media, particularly many computer games, gives people a feeling that violence and sexual excess are not un-normal. Young adults in particular develop a somewhat casual attitude to violence. This attitude is part of the source of the gun craze afflicting youth today. In the past guns were not a common part of the life of city and suburban youth, and mostly thought of for hunting by country youth.

The line between the violence seen in media sources has led to this attitude change.

Therefore we suggest that, like cigarettes, violent media events and computer games carry a warning label before and after the violent media happening. Cigarettes are hazardous to your physical health, media violence should point out that violence is hazardous to one's mental health. To some extent warning messages of this type in the form of ratings do appear in some cases such as movies. But a clear statement on overly violent or sexual content should appear at the beginning and end of TV programs, movies, computer games, and so on.

Eighty Years of Brain Washing

In the approximately eighty years since the beginning of talking films and the subsequent emergence of other powerful media sources the American people have been transformed from a sedate, morally conservative society to a society with more guns, more violence, more crime, more sexual misbehavior, and more broken homes and badly raised children. We can attribute many causes to this trend but the one that stands out is the media. The social behavior in Hollywood and others media centers has been transferred to the majority of the American people with increasingly disastrous consequences. Knowing the effect of media propaganda and brain washing in totalitarian countries starting with Nazi Germany and proceeding through the Korean War and beyond it is clear that the constant bombardment of the media – oriented as it is towards sex and violence is the primary culprit. To remedy the ill wind of the media we must proceed carefully and maintain freedom of the press and freedom of speech while quelling the glorification of sex, violence and sensationalism that are the hallmark of the media today.

Those who doubt the influence of the media should consider the vast amounts of money spent by advertisers and politicians to influence the public. Does anyone believe that they are advertising if the media did not strongly influence viewers?

7. Crime, Security, Terrorism, and Prisons

Criminal Activity

Criminal activity in the US is on the increase despite the apparent decrease in crime in crime statistics. The reason for the discrepancy is fourfold: 1) the increase in subtle crime – criminal activity that does not off alarm bells because it is "small" crime – petty theft of small items, petty assaults, minor beatings, extortion, theft and return of cars, and so on that do not lead to police complaints or investigations; 2) the increasing cleverness of criminals who use tactics similar to terrorists – hit and run tactics, cell phones and other equipment to escape the police;[11] 3) an increase in violent retaliation for people who report crime to the police – retaliation both to the informer and the informer's family[12] – result - a code of silence; 4) corruption in law enforcement officers – some are members of gangs – makes reporting crimes dangerous.

So crime statics decrease while the petty and major violence experienced by Americans increase. And the crimes are hidden from the authorities. A number of cities, towns and counties are controlled by organized crime elements. These

---

[1111] In some cases criminals track police cars and "phone ahead" to perpetrators of a crime alerting them to the imminent arrival of police vehicles.

[12] An informer's spouse, children and relatives – even if far away - are often the victims of retaliation. No mercy is shown. Cell phone retaliation "courtesies" are often exchanged by gangs in different locations.

elements are increasingly coordinating their activities using modern telecommunications devices such as cell phones.

The only possible solution to these increasingly hidden crimes, often using high tech equipment, is counterinsurgency measures adapted to conform to the laws of the United States with fast response police teams composed of police with protected identities – the police are often victims of retaliation too. These teams should operate at the state and federal levels.

Drugs and Crime - Legalization

In 1900 the American population of approximately 100,000,000 people numbered 500,000 addicts in the population. The principal drug was morphine. Cocaine was known and used. It was even an ingredient in Coca Cola at the time. In response to drug addiction laws were passed prohibiting the use of drugs without prescriptions.

Since then the variety and amount of illegal drugs has mushroomed. Today we have many more addicts and recreational drug users. These drugs are manufactured here or brought into the country in massive quantities. Like alcohol prohibition making drug usage illegal has not eliminated the problem – it has merely provided criminal organizations a very lucrative source of large revenues, corrupted law enforcement, and caused a massive crime wave to pay for highly priced drugs. Drug prohibition is not only a failure it is the source of most of the crime in the US.

This situation can only be remedied, much like alcohol prohibition was remedied, by repeal of drug prohibition and the creation of government owned and operated stores for drugs that sell drugs to individuals with a doctor's prescription[13] at a high price that is much less their current street price. If implemented it would soon end the illegal drug trade and the crimes committed by drug users to support their habits. It would also sharply curtail police corruption. Thus the benefits are manifold for society[14] and for drug addicts. To those who would argue drug usage is immoral we invite them to consider the current scene with the crime, violence and degradation it entails. This approach would also enable families and individuals to seek help to escape from drug addiction without themselves committing criminal offenses by helping.

Drug usage would have laws similar to those that apply to alcohol consumption: not while driving vehicles and not in public display would apply to drug consumption – perhaps with stiffer penalties.

The controlled legalization of drugs is not likely to increase the population of drug users. Drugs are so readily available now that all who want to buy drugs can do so.

The control of drug sales by the federal government would have a secondary benefit as a source of significant revenues much needed by the government. While this consequence might offend some ("making dirty money off of drug sales") the above stated benefits for society, and particularly the freedom from fear engendered by a much lower crime rate, will more than justify this proposal.

---

[13] Fraudulent abuse of prescriptions and harassment of physicians should be felony crimes with substantial fines and prison terms.

[14] Another benefit that is not as shameful as it might seem is the revenue that would be generated for government by drug stores. Due to the prevalence of closed and almost empty post offices the federal government could quickly ramp up a drug store network.

Freeing the Drug Addicts in Prison

One year after the federal legal drug system was set up it would be appropriate to release all druggies in prisons that have only used drugs – on perhaps five year probation with a return to jail if caught in crime. Convicts who engaged in small time drug sales would have their cases reviewed and possibly be similarly paroled. Major drug dealers would serve their terms since their crime was great.

A corollary benefit of the release of minor drug offenders from prison is a significant saving in prison costs. The cost of keeping a person in prison ranges up to $40,000 per year. Freeing perhaps 250,000 prisoners would result in cost savings of up to ten billion dollars *per year* or 100 billion dollars in ten years.

The Cost of Prisons

The United States has approximately 3,000,000 people in prisons – one percent of the population. At $40,000 per year the cost is $120,000,000,000 or 120 billion dollars *per year*. In ten years the cost is 1.2 trillion dollars – an amount that makes it a significant factor in the Federal and state financial picture.

We cannot free these people. The vast majority are a danger to society. However, it is clear that the US should find ways to reduce the costs of prisons – prison expenses are siphoning money away from far more important activities of the US and state governments.

One approach that makes sense is to reduce unnecessary costs. One can't reduce the cost of guards; one can't starve the prisoners. The only humane possibility for cost reduction is in the perks that seem to be present in many prisons. One perk that is particularly outrageous and should be eliminated is gym facilities.

Gyms are being used by inmates to strengthen their muscles for fighting inside prison and to help their criminal activities after they are released. We do not need ogres produced in prison gyms. If prisoners want exercise facilities they can do pushups etc. in their cells and expensive gym facilities could be replaced with low cost, low upkeep outdoor tracks. Running is a good exercise and does not create muscle bound thugs.

Another method of reducing the number and expense of prison inmates is a greater humane use of the death penalty for murderers and others committing horrendous crimes, and, in addition, three time losers who have committed serious felony crimes. In suggesting this method the following points must be recognized:

1. While many people think the death penalty is punishment and a form of vengeance, the more important purpose of the death penalty is the removal from society of dangerous individuals who could never be let loose upon society in a society that cannot afford to support these individuals indefinitely. In the past when life was more precarious, and resources barely met the needs of a society, the only reasonable recourse was to put murderers and criminals that committed serious crimes to death. The US is not far from being a society that is hard pressed to take care of all its children and needy adults. Under these circumstances the death penalty for murderers and hardened criminals is justified. It is true some innocent people may be convicted of murder. One can only reply that they are the exceptions. Many innocent people die in war yet wars continue. We can only feel

sympathy for the few individuals that are executed although innocent. But the death penalty, which is justified for the vast majority of guilty and convicted murderers, should not be abandoned if an occasional miscarriage of justice happens.

2. People convicted of murder have many opportunities to seek reversal of the conviction. Many appeal situations last for years. Thus the possibility of the innocent being executed for murder is minimal these days.

3. Three time losers are individuals convicted three times of serious felonies. Clearly these individuals are a great danger to society and cannot be set free or taught to behave. It is unlikely that a person would be wrongfully convicted of a major felony on three occasions. So a three time loser is clearly not likely to be innocent. Under these conditions the execution of three times losers to remove them from society and lower the substantial costs of an indefinite prison life is justified. The US can no longer support seriously criminal inmates.

For these reasons the death penalty should be used. All babies start out as innocents. Some grow up under horrid circumstances or bad influences to become murderers or hardened criminals. They have our sympathy but the greater good of society justifies the death penalty for them.

One must also remember that the execution of murderers and three time losers does have a significant *deterrent effect* on individuals contemplating serious crime or murder. Unfortunately some misguided individuals seek to avoid punishment by surreptitiously committing crimes. One hopes that these criminals will come to justice in God's good time.

Terrorists

Terrorists who are citizens or permanent residents of the US should be tried with due process in courts for their crimes. They are not soldiers so the Geneva Convention does not apply. They are best viewed as saboteurs and spies. These categories of crime should be handled by the civil criminal code unless they are members of the US military. In this case they should be tried in military court.

Terrorists who are foreign citizens and not permanent residents of the US are a problem. Many are being held at Guantanamo Bay in jail cells. Almost all are hardened terrorist criminals. They should not be tried in American civilian courts or military courts to avoid perverting our justice system.

We do not want to support them permanently in expensive prison facilities without a fair trial process. The only fair solution to this dilemma appears to be one that was used by Fidel Castro. Some years ago he released prisoners who committed serious crimes and sent them in boats to the US who then had the burden of dealing with them.

We suggest that the prisoners in Guantanamo be transported in lots of fifty or a hundred to the Iraqi border with Iran and freed to enter Iran. If Iran denies them entry then Iran will lose face in the Arab world for turning away its brother Arabs. If Iran accepts them, then the US is released from the expense and burden of their imprisonment. To those who feel these terrorists will resume terrorist activities against the US we say that Iran is filled with such people now. So adding a few more terrorists to Iran's hostile population will not damage US security. It will perhaps give us good publicity in the world. Thus America has nothing to lose by this action and much to gain in terms of reduced expenses and likely increased good will in the world (and especially in Europe where Guantanamo is deplored.)

Prison Abuses

Prisons in the US are very often hell holes where young, old and weak prisoners are subject to abuse and cruelty that seems to test the limits of the constitutional ban on "cruel and unusual punishment." Many people feel that prisoners are getting their just deserts in prison.

But one must realize that the net effect of this process of abuse and degradation, when prisoners are released after serving their time, are individuals who are physically and/or psychologically unable to cope with society. They then become outcasts who often turn to crime or drugs or both. Society thus suffers from the abuse to which the prison system turns a blind eye.

Therefore we suggest that serious prison reform is needed – not to coddle prisoners – but to encourage them to become good citizens after they are released. Better job training and basic education are needed then are presently available. In addition prison security should add extra guards to clamp down on prisoner abuse, fighting, and gangs.

A Major Misconception about Prisons

Many people think that a prisoner gets his/her just deserts in prison. For example, a Pennsylvania judge of my acquaintance would tell defendants in child molestation, rape and abuse cases that they would "Get theirs" at sentencing after conviction. The judge felt that the prison inmates would punish new prison inmates in these sorts of cases. However, an ex-con who I unknowingly hired to do work on my house, and found to have been in prison, told me that the judge's opinion was wrong based on his experience. He said that there were so many child molesters in his prison that they formed a social group and sat around telling stories about their child abuse crimes. If this is generally true, and it may well be, then prisons are educating inmates for further crime upon release. Thus the need for the training and the rehabilitation of convicts before release.

Excess Federal Appeals by Criminals

We often hear of murder cases, in which a person is convicted of murder and sentenced to death, with the execution of the death penalty delayed for many years (ten year delays have sometimes occurred). The constitution guarantees a person to a fair and speedy trial. Implicit in that guarantee is the expectation that the sentence will be promptly given and meted out. Long delays in the execution of a sentence would seem to be contrary to the intent of the authors of the constitution.

Thus it would seem reasonable to reform the appeal process so that delays in executions for the appeals process are limited to perhaps two years in fairness to all concerned. This would help ease the problems of our overloaded court system and be a significant savings to the tax payer. Today in many small cities and towns known criminals can often commit crimes and "get away with them" because the city or town cannot afford the expense of lengthy court proceedings. This type of situation demands that the court process be streamlined.

8. Poverty and Unemployment

The problems of poverty and unemployment in America have been with us for many generations. Many solutions have been proposed. Some have been enacted – particularly in the Great Depression. Today we face a similar economic crisis whose dimensions are becoming known despite well-meant efforts by our political leaders to put a brave face on the situation in an effort to talk our way through our problems.

These efforts are good. But we must realize that we shall always have poverty and unemployment to a greater or lesser extent due to the nature of Mankind and the nature of the economic cycle. Thus our best hope is to find ways to ameliorate poverty and unemployment so that the suffering they engender will be minimized.

Poverty in America

The number of people in poverty has soared in recent years due to a large increase in unemployment, a large increase in underemployment, and the common transition of many workers from higher paying jobs to low pay jobs. The hardships endured by people who are newly poor or borderline poor are more or less known. But efforts to reduce this problem are piecemeal at best and the attention of the American people is shaped by the media to ignore the problem except when crime or disastrous events make it "newsworthy." Perhaps the only bright spot in the presidential conventions of 2012 was the comment of Mr. Clint

Eastwood that he was very concerned about an America with twenty-four million unemployed. His concern was not forcefully echoed by other speeches at these conventions.

So it is fair to say that poverty is pretty much ignored by people who are not in poverty – except for short face-saving comments.

Can we Remedy Poverty?

There have been many attempts to ameliorate the welfare of those in poverty. Some attempts such as unemployment benefits have helped. But unemployment benefits eventually end while unemployment continues. In contrast some European countries such as Germany have a strong continuing unemployment benefits program. Some will think that such a program will encourage laziness and the avoidance of serious job searches. To that I can only reply that anyone who has gone to a US unemployment office with their typical long lines and dreary atmosphere (as I have on one occasion) will see that no one prefers unemployment benefits to a *real* job.

Other programs such as housing the long term unemployed in motels and hotels rather than have them homeless on the street are an expensive[15] and flawed approach to the problem of poverty.

---

[15] For example the poor in Westchester County, NY are often housed in motels at an expense to the taxpayer of upwards of $100 per day. Motel room living for families is hardly comfortable and creates problems for their children. The Westchester situation is not uncommon in other parts of the country.

The Rumford Solution for the Poor

Count Rumford a famous physicist of the 19th century implemented a solution for the poor in his city in Germany that bears investigation as a possible solution for today's America. He took unused factories, converted them to living quarters and workshops where the poor could live and work, and make money to eventually escape from poverty. The Rumford Solution worked well.

In America the closest we have come to the Rumford Solution was low cost housing developments for low income people. These developments were often not well maintained or properly policed with the result that they became "new" crime-ridden public housing "slums."

It seems reasonable to develop a federal Rumford program that would take large "empty" factories and convert them to a set of studio apartments for singles and full size apartments for families together with a large area reserved for shops and small assembly sub-factories that could provide employment to the residents. There are many small companies and startups that could benefit from employing the poor at lower wages. The poor in these Rumford establishments could save or spend the pay they receive as part of a startup lifestyle of employment. The mistakes of low cost housing developments could be avoided by requiring tenants keep their homes clean and orderly, and by a resident "police force" that could maintain the safety and security of the residents. Remedial night courses could be offered to provide basic reading, writing and math skills to help them in job seeking in the future.

This idea can be extended for the case of the many young single, footloose unemployed by creating work camps for them to rebuild the nation's parks' infrastructure and forests. They would receive food, lodging, pay and an opportunity to learn reading, writing and math if they should need it. Programs such as this program are similar to the Depression Era Civilian Conservation Corps (CCC), which were successful in helping America recover.

Help the Children

Many children throughout the United States go to school hungry and/or do not receive nutritious meals at home. School lunch programs and school breakfast programs are currently available in many areas and states. Since children are the future of America it seems that the government should create a national breakfast and lunch program for children in elementary school. The food should be nutritious and should not emulate fast food and pizza, which are known to be the sources of bad diets that later lead to unhealthy diets for teens and adults. Naturally the food served should be appealing to young appetites.

A small federal research program to determine healthy, appealing breakfast and lunch menus should be initiated that has the major goal of providing the necessary daily requirements for protein, vitamins, and minerals required by elementary school children. Thus children will have the proper daily nutrition no matter what their family dinners are. The tendency to use federal surplus commodities such as peanut butter should be carefully scrutinized since peanut butter, for example, can tend to promote obesity if taken in larger quantities.[16]

---

[16] After seeing the relatively large number of obese children on Indian reservations the author wonders if it might be connected to the federal surplus food given to the Indians. A study of this potential issue would appear appropriate given the centuries of bad treatment of Indians in America.

Help Families

Many young, and not so young, people marry without a sound understanding of how to get along in marriage and how to properly raise children. This problem is the result of the development of a youth culture (previously discussed) and the decided dislike of learning the child rearing and domestic routines of their parents – a failure in the transmittal of knowledge between generations – relatively new in America – but a source of major difficulties for young people later in life.

In view of the impact of this problem[17] it seems reasonable to suggest that marriage counselors and child care counselors should be available under the expanded all-ages Medicare program that we advocated earlier. In addition the mothers (and fathers of all first newborns) should be required to take a parenting course at the hospital where the child was born (or a nearby hospital if the baby was not born in a hospital.)

In order to ease the financial burden of children a Children's Exchange should be created in all villages, towns, and cities that is funded by state governments that allows parents to buy and sell clean children's used clothes, and toys, in good repair. The Exchange should make a small profit on each sale to partially support its operation.

Unemployment in America

The unemployment problem in America can best be solved by redeveloping a competitive domestic economy. The wage differential based tariff proposed in chapter 1 is the best

---

[17] There are fairly frequent news stories about parents killing or mistreating their children. These stories are merely the tip of a large iceberg of bad parenting.

approach to creating a level international playing field that will enable American industry to revive.

Who Pays for these Programs

Most of the cost of the programs advocated in this chapter can be funded by restructuring existing federal and state programs. The remaining needed funds should be funded by the substantial revenues obtained from the wage differential tariffs, and perhaps by a relatively small increase in the federal debt, in view of their importance to the welfare of the people.

9. Pollution and Waste Disposal

The United States, and the world, face massive pollution and waste disposal problems. The pollution problem has reached the stage where the "standard" solution for pollution – dilution in bodies of water no longer works. Water bodies have generally reached a level of pollution that the health of people who use water for drinking and washing is starting to be strongly affected. Even the ultimate bodies of water for dilution – the oceans – all of them except the Arctic – have noticeable pollution in the obvious form of plastic refuse and detritus. More subtle forms of dilution by poisonous substances as mercury are increasing.[18]

Subtle forms of pollution in toxic waste dumps on land and in water supplies are causing birth defects, cancer and other diseases. Wholesale pollution over the past 100 years in Russia has led to a 50% birth defect rate in newborn infants. In the United States many toxic waste dumps still exist and many are as yet unknown. It is not uncommon for housing developments to be built on covered toxic dumps. One case with which I am familiar is a town where many homes were built on or near toxic dumps. It is

---

[18] Mercury poisoning in particular will increase dramatically due to the high price of gold. Mercury is used in gold production and the high price will lead to increasing mining activity with a resulting surge in mercury in seawater making fish dangerous to eat in quantity. Since fish is a worldwide mainstay of the human diet from Norway to Africa, and a very healthy food, mercury and other pollutants will affect the world – including third world countries such as Ghana where it is the major protein in the country's diet.

no surprise that the town has an excessive number of autistic children and children with learning disabilities.[19]

Is there a Solution?

Yes, but the solution will be costly. Is it worth it? Yes if you value your life, your family's lives and your children's lives. The solution can be described by:

1. Every product, including mined materials such as gold and coal, should have a surcharge for disposal of its associated waste and pollution to pay for its cleanup. To some extent this is already done for some products such as soda cans. It should be done for all mined and manufactured products.

2. The resulting revenue should be used to find and clean up all toxic waste dumps, to provide for the disposal of newly created pollutants, to create and upgrade waste disposal facilities, and to eliminate the discharge of untreated waste into water bodies including the oceans.

3. This surcharge should be collected on all sales of products and paid to the federal government for a national effort with some monies distributed to states for part of the cleanup.

---

[19] I learned this from a teacher of autistic children in that town who spoke in a low, guarded tone of voice. An unmentionable, I gather. In another conversation I heard a similar story from a woman who was house hunting, and was warned against buying a house in a certain development by a real estate agent because it was locally known to have been consciously built on a toxic waste site by a developer.

4. Strict penalties should be set including large fines and felony jail time for people who knowingly create, or conceal the existence, of toxic waste dumps.

5. A federal agency should supervise this effort and determine fair pricing of the environmental surcharge. Companies could pay the surcharge monies collected with their income tax payments.

The Price

The price for a cleaner environment is the increased cost of almost all items due to the environmental surcharge. This surcharge will lower demand, especially for very polluting products, and thus have an economic impact. But the expenditure of these funds for environmental cleanup and improvement will help the economy and mitigate the ill effects of increased prices.

The Benefits

The benefits of this proposed program will be apparent for this generation and future generations in the form of a healthier population and a more attractive environment. Little as it may sound to some, it is the key to a bright future for Mankind.

More importantly it will strongly stimulate industry and manufacturing to redesign products to have lesser pollution impact, and to collect their waste products to reduce disposal problems. It will lead to products that are more disposable without environmental deterioration. For example, milk companies might return to using glass milk bottles rather than plastic ones. Glass can be disposed of easily. Plastic cannot – as the plastic floating in the oceans reminds us.

It might also stimulate other governments such as Russia and China to clean up their environments. Their pollution is part of a worldwide problem. For example, Chinese air pollution reaches the continental United States and contributes to poorer air quality. As the Arctic warms one can expect an increase in "over the pole" pollution.

10. Exporting Technology

Recent news articles have highlighted the issue of industrial espionage of trade secrets and proprietary information and data by foreign countries. Much of the espionage has been through the Internet. Foreign "hackers" work their way through the firewalls[20] protecting American company information and scoop up important data that gave American companies a competitive edge in world and domestic markets.

Trade secret and proprietary information espionage also take place in the old fashioned way – through agents and the extraction of information from employees.

But these mechanisms for "forcibly" obtaining technology and trade secrets have an open counterpart in world trade relations. Foreign nations can often simply buy products and produce "knock offs." The fashion industry has had this issue for many years. The problem originates in more vital industries such as the aircraft and the military industries where America's technical advantages are vital to American export strength, and more importantly, to America's defense.

---

[20] One of the author's friends was the leading "hacking" expert at a major American computer software company. He said, "I can work my way through any walls protecting a computer! I do it wall by wall." This statement appears to be true given the great success of hackers, domestic and foreign, in penetrating not only domestic company computers but also military and government computers to extract information. The US government and private companies are attempting to forestall these efforts. But it seems that their efforts have not been entirely successful.

If we export technology to foreign countries by exporting products that they can copy, then we are faced with the dilemma of how to prevent such exports from being technology exports. It does not seem possible to do this unless one deliberately puts "Rube Goldberg" devices in the products that do nothing but serve to make the product more difficult to understand and copy. To the author's knowledge very few companies use this ploy.[21]

The US government does have restrictions in place for weapons sold to foreign countries to preclude potentially hostile countries from obtaining the weapons and making copies – or worse improved versions.

Perhaps the only solution to making it less likely that US industry will export vital technology to foreign countries is a stricter licensing requirement whereby a license is required for exporting products and technology in areas of national interest. This type of licensing requirement is in place for military technology. It should be expanded to include computer software and hardware technology, aircraft technology, and so on.

In addition the practice of American companies to "outsource" important technology to take advantage of lower foreign labor costs should be carefully scrutinized and regulated. If the US outsources the vast majority of its computer chip production to foreign companies (indeed to companies in countries that are potential enemies) then the US military would be unable to carry on a sustained war such as in WW I, WW II and Vietnam. If the US outsources its software industry, as it is

---

[21] This author did in his pioneering Desktop Publishing Company – Blaha Software Inc. – since he had a competitive edge for a while in laser printer interfaces in the 1980's. It was necessary in order to make competition by much larger companies by reverse engineering our software more difficult.

currently doing to a large extent,[22] who will program for the US if the outsource country becomes hostile. Massive outsourcing puts foreign countries in a position to blackmail the US. There is no shortage of potential hostile countries. We know of the obvious ones: North Korea and Iran. But there are signs that Russia is becoming expansionary to recover its lost power. China is making major inroads into oil-rich Central Asia through economic efforts such as building oil pipelines and roads, and by supporting local Communist parties financially. The US has been forced out of Central Asian countries by Chinese instigated local agitators.

We conclude that the US should also regulate outsourcing of potentially vital industries to potentially hostile nations.

---

[22] Outsourcing highly skilled jobs creates another problem for the US. In many fields of endeavor the more senior workers know "tips of the trade" or "lore" that enables them to produce exceptional output. Computer programming is a perfect example. Typically new programmers learn the tricks of the trade from older programmers. For example, when I worked at Bell Laboratories new or junior programmers informally obtained advice and help from the senior programmers who were called "gurus." If programming is outsourced to a foreign country then new programmers in the US will eventually be unable to learn from gurus. This guru gap could happen in a short period of time – perhaps ten years. Then the foreign country would have a technical advantage over US programmers should the US revive its software industry in the future – either due to hostilities or the arrival of an opportunity for the US software industry to successfully compete due to a changed cost of labor situation. Thus outsourcing of high tech industries may lead to an unwelcome dependence on foreign industries that would be difficult to reverse.

11. Space, Research, and Defense

Space

The American space program, NASA, has had many successes starting with the first American in orbit and the first man on the moon. The NASA space program is built exclusively at present on the use of rockets using chemical fuels – chemical rockets. Early in its history, in the 1960's, other methods for traveling to space such as nuclear rockets and space guns a la Jules Verne were considered. The prototype nuclear rocket program, NERVA, was designed and a prototype engine was built in the 1960's. This program projected it could put a man on Mars by 1978. The Nixon administration cancelled the project for budget reasons. The space gun program examined big Navy guns as a method of shooting payloads into space cheaply. This program was cancelled because it used more or less standard Navy gun technology. That type of gun, when scaled up to shoot large payloads, became inefficient.

Consequently the US (and Russia) came to rely solely on chemical rockets. This rocket technology has now matured to the point where private industry can build and fly rockets carrying payloads into space and NASA, and private telecommunications companies, have started using private rocket companies for transport to space.

In a recent book this author suggested new forms of space guns that could send large amounts of cargo into space using new gun designs. I also proposed new reactor and nuclear rocket designs.[23] The author hopes that NASA will seriously consider and pursue building space guns and nuclear rockets (which can be safely built and used in space.)

The cost of this program can be covered by the current NASA budget of 18 billion dollars by re-prioritizing its program.

When starting a major enterprise it is important to build the support infrastructure before pursuing the enterprise's goals. NASA has been using costly rocket technology because it works and because there is long term experience in its use.

We suggest that current programs to explore Mars and the outer solar system be suspended (unless they are so far along that little cost savings would accrue) until a space gun and nuclear rocket infrastructure can be built. Mars, the oceans of Titan and other expensive projects can be deferred for ten years or so in favor of building a superior, more cost effective infrastructure based on space guns and nuclear rockets. The phenomena on Mars and the outer planets will be little changed, if at all, in ten or fifteen years.

It appears that a major driving force for these programs is the search for alien life. The results of this search, if successful, will impact on our view of ourselves and the universe but does not appear to have any practical impact on science. The most likely type of life that will be found is small microbes at best. The earth still has countless numbers of undiscovered microbes extending from the earth's surface to depths of several kilometers. Alien microbes can be expected to only differ in details from earth microbes.

---

[23] See Blaha (2013).

The development of a space infrastructure as proposed by Blaha (2013) would eventually enable colonies to be established on the moon, Mars and on other bodies in the solar system. Its cost effectiveness would make the development of trade with space colonies feasible. See Blaha (2013) for a detailed proposal that could be funded by a NASA budget that looks to the future from a long term perspective – not as a bunch of single shot exploratory projects that only seek immediate, small scientific rewards.

Research

Government research is broadly based and has been very successful both scientifically and practically for the benefit of the US and the world.

Under current tight budgets support for research should continue without cutbacks for federal deficit reduction. Research should be especially fostered in medicine, solid state physics and other branches of physics that have good prospects for energy savings, miniaturization of technology to help reduce waste, and labor savings to make the economy more efficient and competitive in world markets.

Defense

A strong defense is necessary in an increasingly hostile world. Potential trouble spots include: Siberia (Russia vs. China), the Arctic (a mix of nations with conflicting claims to Arctic oil and minerals), Antarctica, Africa (many ongoing conflicts), the Mideast (conflicts and growing anti-Americanism in most Muslim countries together with the Iranian nuclear threat), the Black Sea countries (Russia is seeking hegemony over its former satellites, the Ukraine and Georgia), Central Asia (Chinese expansionism in these oil rich countries), the Koreas, and South America (especially an unstable Venezuela and Columbia).

Given these potential areas of conflict the US must maintain its defense posture. Instead of reducing the size of the Army it should be taking advantage of the unemployment problem to increase its size and quality.

Further the shift to larger and larger ships – particularly aircraft carriers – should be moderated in favor of a smaller, more numerous, more mobile fleet of lower cost ships and aircraft. In war a large fleet of smaller ships and aircraft would be more flexible, and be better able to withstand losses. In addition, in a protracted conflict it would be easier to replace losses with smaller ships and less complex aircraft.

If we go to a program consisting of a small number of very large aircraft carriers then the loss of a carrier becomes a major tragedy. As the Chinese foreign minister said recently, "We are not worried about a large new American aircraft carrier. We could neutralize it with a 1,000 fishing boats armed with rockets."

So we suggest a smaller, faster fleet of ships and aircraft – well-armed but not extremely expensive – will better serve the US for defense.

Postscript

The overall program that we advocate in this book will help create a resurgent America second to none with hope in the future.[24] It will justify the blood and treasure spent by past generations of Americans in war and peace. The time for action is the present!

---

[24] The personal comments and anecdotes that I have made in this book are not particular to me. They reflect a general situation or condition.

REFERENCES

Blaha, S., 2009a, *Bright Stars, Bright Universe* (Pingree-Hill Publishing, Auburn, NH, 2009).

_____, 2009b, *To Far Stars and Galaxies: Second Edition of Bright Stars, Bright Universe*   (Pingree-Hill Publishing, Auburn, NH, 2009).

_____, 2010, *SuperCivilizations: Civilizations as Superorganisms* (McMann-Fisher Publishing, Auburn, NH, 2010).

_____, 2011c, *All the Universe! Faster Than Light Tachyon Quark Starships & Particle Accelerators with the LHC as a Prototype Starship Drive Scientific Edition* (Pingree-Hill Publishing, Auburn, NH, 2011).

_____, 2013, *Multi-Stage Space Guns, Micro-Pulse Nuclear Rockets, and Faster-Than-Light Quark-Gluon Ion Drive Starships* (Blaha Research, Auburn, NH, 2013).

INDEX

age discrimination, 27, 28
aircraft carriers, 79
aircraft companies, 11
alien life, 77
appeal process, 61
bankrupt America, 13
birth defect rate, 69
Black Jack Pershing, 45
Border patrol, 44
brain washing, 51
bread and circuses, 23
buyouts, 28
cartels, 3
chemical rockets, 76
child abuse, 32, 33, 61
Children's Exchange, 67
Chinese Coprosperity Sphere, 15
civil unrest, 25
class structure, 2
college education, 20, 35
computer chips, 1
computer programming, 16, 17
corruption, 24, 25, 47, 53, 55
Count Rumford, 65
crime reporting, 49
crime statistics, 53
criminal activity, 53
death penalty, 57
defect free chips, 1
drug cartels, 25
Eastwood, Clint, 64
education, 35
education loans, 7
entitlement, 23, 47
entry level jobs, 7
federal debt, 21, 68
first strike, 17

Foreign Aid, 8
Great Depression, viii, 2, 19, 63
growing population, 26
Guantanamo, 59
gurus, 75
hackers, 73
have not's, 3
health insurance, 3, 11, 18, 19, 31, 33
Hispanic Americans, 42
housing, 64
housing developments, 65
illegal drugs, 54
illegal immigrants, 43
immigration, 41, 44
import duties, 3
India, 42
industrial espionage, 73
infrastructure, space, 78
ink jet printers, 1
Internet, 50
job security, 18, 19
juvenile delinquents, 36
knock offs, 73
labor camps, 44
Lalaland, 50
low wage countries, 3
marriage counselors, 67
Mars, 76, 77, 78
Medicare, 27, 28, 29, 30, 31, 32, 33, 34, 67
mercury poisoning, 69
middle class, 19
military industry, 11
monetary policy, 15
Most Favored Nation, 1, 2
NASA, 76, 77, 78

National Achievement Test, 38
Navy guns, 76
NERVA, 76
North Korea, 15, 17
nuclear rocket program, 76
nursing facility, 30
Obamacare, 27, 30, 31, 32
oil rich Central Asia, 14
outsourcing, 7, 8
outsourcing industries, 16
Pancho Villa, 45
pensions, 11, 18
pollution, 69
poverty, 19, 63, 64
prisons, 56, 60
public education, 37
rare earth metals, 16
rewarding teachers, 36
robber baron practices, 14
Rome, 24
Rube Goldberg, 74
Rumford Solution, 65
skilled workers, 16, 35
small business, 24
small business startup, 24
Social Security, 18, 24, 27, 28, 34
space gun program, 76
standard of living, 11
strategic goods, 16
sustained war, 3
Swiss franc, 22

tariff on imports, 2
teacher bonus program, 38
terrorists, 59
theft, 20, 25, 53
three time losers, 58
toxic waste dumps, 69
trade deficit, 4
trade imbalance, 2
trade surpluses, 11
underemployed, 19, 41
underreport crime, 20
unemployment, 3, 4, 11, 19, 35,
    63, 64, 67, 79
unemployment benefits, 3
unemployment benefits program,
    64
unfair trade practices, 15
upward mobility, 20
Value Added Tax, 11
violence, 20, 38, 47, 48, 49, 50, 51,
    53, 55
visiting nurses, 32
vitamin C, 14
wage differential duties, 8, 11
wage differential import duty, 5
warning label, 51
waste disposal, 69
water problem, 41
weaponry, 3
white collar job, 36
youth culture, 47, 67

About the Author

Stephen Blaha is an internationally known physicist with interests in Science, the Arts, and Technology. He had an Alfred P. Sloan Foundation scholarship in college. He received his Ph.D. in Physics from Rockefeller University. He has served on the faculties of several major universities. He was also a Member of the Technical Staff at Bell Laboratories, a manager at the Boston Globe Newspaper, a Director at Wang Laboratories, and President of Blaha Software Inc. and of Janus Associates Inc. (NH).

Among other achievements he was a co-discoverer of the "r potential" for heavy quark binding developing the first (and still the only demonstrable) non-abelian gauge theory with an "r" potential; first suggested the existence of topological structures in superfluid He-3; first proposed Yang-Mills theories would appear in condensed matter phenomena with non-scalar order parameters; first developed a grammar-based formalism for quantum computers and applied it to elementary particle theories; first developed a new form of quantum field theory without divergences (thus solving a major 60 year old problem that enabled a unified theory of the Standard Model and Quantum Gravity without divergences to be developed); first developed a formulation of complex General Relativity based on analytic continuation from real space-time; first developed a generalized non-homogeneous Robertson-Walker metric that enabled a quantum theory of the Big Bang to be developed without singularities at t = 0; first generalized Cauchy's theorem and Gauss' theorem to complex, curved multi-dimensional spaces; received Honorable Mention in the Gravity Research Foundation Essay Competition in 1978; first developed a physically acceptable theory of faster-than-light particles; first showed a universe with three complex spatial dimensions is icosahedral; first derived a composition of extrema method in the Calculus of Variations; first quantitatively suggested that inflationary periods in the history of the universe were not needed; first proved Gödel's Theorem implies Nature must be quantum; provided a new alternative to the Higgs Mechanism, and Higgs particles, to generate masses; first showed how to resolve logical paradoxes including Gödel's Undecidability Theorem by developing Operator Logic and Quantum Operator Logic; first developed a quantitative harmonic oscillator-like model of the life cycle, and interactions, of civilizations; first showed how equations describing superorganisms also apply to civilizations; and first developed an axiomatic derivation of the forms of The Standard Model with WIMPs from geometry – space-time properties – The faster than light Standard Model.

He has had a major impact on a succession of elementary particle theories: his Ph.D. thesis (1970), and papers, showed that quantum field theory calculations to all orders in ladder approximations could not give scaling deep inelastic electron-nucleon scattering. He later showed the eigenvalue equation for the fine structure constant α in Johnson-Baker-Willey QED had a zero at $\alpha = 1$ not 1/137 by solving the Schwinger-Dyson equations to all orders in an approximation that agreed with exact results to 8th order in α thus ending interest in this theory. In 1979 at Prof. Ken Johnson's (MIT) suggestion he calculated the proton-neutron mass difference in the MIT bag model and found the result had the wrong sign reducing interest in the bag model. These results all appear in Physical Review papers. In the 2000's he repeatedly pointed out the shortcomings of SuperString theory and showed that The Standard Model's form could be derived from space-time geometry by an extension of Lorentz transformations to faster than light transformations. This deeper space-time basis greatly increases the possibility that it is part of THE fundamental theory.

In the early 1980's Blaha was also a pioneer in the development of UNIX for financial, scientific and Internet applications: benchmarked UNIX versions showing that block size was critical for UNIX performance, developing financial modeling software, starting database benchmarking comparison studies, developing Internet-like UNIX networking (1982) and developing a hybrid shell programming technique (1982) that was a precursor to the PERL programming language. He was also the manager of the AT&T ten-year future products development database. His work helped lead to commercial UNIX on computers such as Sun Micros, IBM AIX minis, and Apple computers.

In the 1980's he pioneered the development of PC Desktop Publishing on laser printers. and was nominated for three "Awards for Technical Excellence" in 1987 by PC Magazine for PC software products that he designed and developed.

In the past ten years Dr. Blaha has written over 35 books on a wide range of topics. Some recent major works are: *From Asynchronous Logic to The Standard Model to Superflight to the Stars, All the Universe!* and *SuperCivilizations: Civilizations as Superorganisms.*

www.ingramcontent.com/pod-product-compliance
Lightning Source LLC
Chambersburg PA
CBHW071057280326
41928CB00050B/2540